THE JUDGMENTS OF
FATHER JUDGE

Thomas Augustine Judge, C.M., M.S.SS.T.

THE JUDGMENTS OF
FATHER JUDGE

A Study of

Very Rev. THOMAS AUGUSTINE JUDGE,
C.M., M.S.SS.T.

Who Founded the Communities of Missionary Servants of the Most Holy Trinity and Missionary Servants of the Most Blessed Trinity

BY

JOACHIM V. BENSON,
M.S.SS.T.

NEW YORK
P. J. KENEDY & SONS
PUBLISHERS

Nihil Obstat:
    ARTHUR J. SCANLAN, S.T.D.
          Censor Librorum

Imprimatur:
    ✠ PATRICK CARDINAL HAYES
          Archbishop of New York

New York
October 8, 1934.

"If it is of God, the work will go on. If it
is not, let it perish immediately."—*Father Judge*.

INTRODUCTION

THIS was the life of Father Judge: that he would do whatever God willed, how and when God willed it. And in obeying the Divine Will as a humble and obedient servant of the Triune God, his aim was "to lead others to a greater eating of the Sacred Body of Christ and a greater drinking of His Precious Blood." There was no middle course or compromise or quibble of conscience. "As God wills It," he would say, and "Let God's Church speak."

It was part of his *credo* not to question the Divine Wishes but to fulfil them. He felt himself but an apprentice in the school of the Master Carpenter, a privileged pupil allowed to contribute his daily labors as outlined in the Eternal and Divine blue print. If he labored well, it was because the Master Carpenter sustained his labors. If he suffered physical or mental pain, the thought of the Man of Sorrows soothed him. If he was more successful than the least of his hopes, then the Providence of God be praised and all honor to His Triune Majesty. He lived convinced that the Cause of All Life quickened his breath, and that when this life should be withdrawn, the All-Merciful One would not be unmerciful to him, the least of His servants.

And each morning above His holy altar, the Son of God looked down from the pure hands of Father Judge and beheld in His apostle the steady growth of faith and hope and charity. Faith that became more profound as Divine Providence exacted its profession. Hope that increased as trials and tribulations demanded greater confidence. And charity that daily bloomed more Christ-like as it sprang from deep wells of love and kindness and sympathy, and overflowed his simple heart in an eagerness to know and love and follow the Great High Priest.

And as he lifted up the cup to the Eternal Father, the chalice filled with the Precious

Blood of His Divine Son, he asked only to be allowed to drain it completely with all the anguish of the Crucified Who spilled it, and too, that he might place within the chalice the sorrows of a redeemed humanity, still burdened with the effects of original sin, struggling toward the Fountain of Life.

It is the opinion of many that he was far in advance of his time. Many openly disagreed with him and opposed his work. But even those who criticised him most severely have not failed to mention his sweet sincerity, his love of God, his solid determination never to swerve from the path of duty as he saw it after council and prayer, and always under the obedience of his superiors.

The following pages are not worthy of the subject. They are being put forward because so many have asked to know more of this man of God. We make no apology for them other than their inadequacy. A true son of Saint Vincent, he followed the teachings of the Apostle of Charity, and gave a modern adaptation to his principles. His early years, even those in the seminary, reveal nothing remarkable, other than that he did ordinary things in an extraordinary way. No one could see in the young and diligent Novice a future Founder of two Religious Communities, one for men, The Missionary Servants of the Most Holy Trinity, and one for women, The Missionary Servants of the Most Blessed Trinity. He himself never dreamed of such a possibility, even after his ordination when he was deeply involved with the Lay Apostolate. But looking back through the years, we see the bright light of the Holy Spirit guiding this humble servant as he climbed upwards by the mighty impulse of love, continually purifying his intentions, doing violence to his will and his body, seeking the God-Man, imitating Him, loving Him and dying with Him every day in his meditations upon the Sacred Passion.

A great saint once said, "Show me someone who forgets himself or herself completely and I will show you someone whom the world

will not willingly forget." Father Judge never
thought of himself. He lived for God and for
his fellow man. His death was the exhaustion
of self. His doctors said they had never seen
a man so completely worn out. Fatigue moved
in on him like the blackness of night, and he
slipped away in God.

Nothing better describes a man than his own
words. For the most part, then, this narrative
is a weaving together of passages from his letters and conferences. A more detailed life of
Father Judge will be published when the All-
Knowing God makes manifest that it all should
be told. For the present we begin with his
ordination, May 27, 1899, and briefly recount
the principal events that led to the formation
of his two Communities. Then, let the simplicity of Father Judge's own words bespeak
his love of God, his Faith, his Hope, and his
Charity.

Saint Vincent has said, "You should not
tread on the heels of Providence, but if Providence opens the way, you should run." Father

Judge truly ran in the pathways of the Lord. Like Saint Vincent he was not swerved by his own will, but followed the direct impulse of his own goodness. Quite often he could not sufficiently complete what he undertook, for he had to go forward with other and more recent enterprises. His zeal knew no bounds where good was concerned. He was acutely sensitive. Sensitive to spiritual truths and love of God. He thought others were like himself— and if you doubted the Providence of God, and asked him to go slowly or to desist from a good work, for any material reason, his eyes would open wide, bewildered, like a child, and he would tell you simply that he could not stop—God didn't will that.

He was bound to be misunderstood. Men of God are always preoccupied with obligations and tormented with superior demands which are beyond their understanding. They have a special vision of their duties. They follow impulses which they must obey. Their natural affection has been transformed into an

[12]

overwhelming love that finds its source and consummation in the Sacred Heart of Jesus. So it was with Father Judge.

He was one of those born for inward conflict and a life of quest. One of those who often must travel alone because he sees wonderful things. And even if the work he began should go no further, the beauty of his noble soul deserves recognition. He placed his hand in God's, and then, like a child, he exclaimed at all the wonderful things that God showed him. In his enthusiasm he tried to tell you how wonderful it was to place your hand in the Hand of God, and to go where He wants you to go.

Like lilies of the valley that have long incensed the shadows with their fragrance, the virtues of Father Judge now lift their modest heads above the leaves of humility. And the noble character of this man of God is revealed more strikingly as his teachings and counsels echo back like sweet music from afar.

THE AUTHOR.

[13]

"This man was instructed in the way of the Lord; and being fervent in spirit, spoke, and taught diligently the things that are of Jesus (*Acts* 18:25).

CHAPTER ONE

Thomas Augustine Judge was ordained a priest of the Congregation of the Mission on May 27, 1899, by Archbishop Patrick John Ryan, at Saint Charles' Seminary, Overbrook, Pennsylvania. The following day, Trinity Sunday, he said his first Mass in Saint Vincent's Seminary, Germantown, Philadelphia, Pennsylvania. For over a year previous he had been a victim of tuberculosis and everyone thought that he would die soon. The young priest did not think so. He sang his first Mass, entered into all the celebrations, and spent the day with his family and friends.

There is no doubt but that he was very sick, and his superiors sent him home with his mother with this remark, "If anyone can cure him, you can. If not, then send him back to us."

He went home and tried as best he might to regain his health. He said Mass at the houses of the Sisters of Charity. He was very weak and had a severe cough. But his will was as strong as his cough, and his faith in Our Blessed Mother stronger than either.

Filled with the principles of Saint Vincent —inflamed with zeal, impulsive, determined, God-loving and God-fearing—we find him in September, 1899, in Saint Vincent's Church, Price Street, Germantown, Philadelphia. His health was still poor, so he was not immediately detailed to the mission band or given exact duties. But his pent-up zeal knew no bounds and he began to work among the Italian poor of the neighborhood. A story is told of that early endeavor to help the poor.

Through his workers he learned of a young girl very ill with tuberculosis who lay, apparently dying, amid conditions that could not have been much worse. Father Judge was himself tubercular, and yet in any danger was perfectly fearless. He visited this poor, frail

creature every day, brought her the Lord God
of Hosts, cheered her, and became the one
bright light in her dreary days. It cost him a
great deal of physical anguish, and almost
every day after visiting his patient he would
ask the druggist next door to fix him something to dispel the feeling of nausea. The
druggist was not a Catholic, though married
to a Catholic girl. He was an honest man
who, having witnessed the self-sacrifice of this
young priest, remarked to his wife one day,
"There's Christianity for you." She made no
reply. They did not discuss religion.

Shortly after, the druggist sent his wife
abroad to regain her lost health. Father
Judge continued his visits to the tubercular
girl. When the wife of the druggist returned
she was surprised to discover that her husband
was studying catechism. Father Judge had
made his first convert, not by a crusade of
words, but by Christlike example. And this
story comes, not indirectly, but vividly with
appreciation by the converted druggist, who

still lives with his wife above the same drug store.

The idea of a spiritualized laity seems to have been with Father Judge constantly. In the first days of his priesthood he did not have a clear concept of just what it would lead to, but he was willing to be guided by the Holy Ghost. He saw then the tremendous power of the laity in assisting the hierarchy in their mission to teach all nations.

"Did you ever think of gathering children on the street and bringing them to Mass," he asked a group of women one day, "or seeking out some poor lost sheep and guiding him or her to the confessional and to the Communion rail? Do you know there are hundreds of children of Catholic parents unbaptized, and many more uninstructed in our Holy Faith? Do you realize there are countless homes where the parents have never been married by the priest? And did you ever think that by your prudent sympathy and patient kindness in going from home to

[20]

home you could bring these souls to Christ?"

All through his life he cried,

"Save the child and you save all." And again, "What you propose to do, especially for the children, is a Christlike, a divine work—quickly to glide in between the child and seduction to threaten the tempter. What a work that is, and then with the patience and kindness of the Heart of Christ to win back to the Church those who are wayward."

About 1903 he was appointed to the regular mission band domiciled at Saint Vincent's Church, Germantown. His intensity as a mission worker soon became evident. He was a marvelous talker and he felt it was his duty to preach. It made no difference to him where he preached. God was everywhere and He should be talked of everywhere. Whenever he felt that there was an opportunity to tell someone of the Unknown God he did not let that opportunity go unheeded.

Once in later years while sitting in a crowded theatre in Phoenix City, Alabama, waiting for the children's annual Christmas play to begin, he suddenly nudged his companion and said, "Ask me to say a few words." His companion was at a loss to understand, and replied, "But, Father, no one said to." "That's all right," he said decisively, "you ask me to say a few words." What matter that the theatre was hot, and that of the three or four hundred packed in, not more than twenty were Catholics? What matter the darkness and that people were impatient because the lights would not function? What matter that his companion thought he might be shouted down? What was there to do? "Well, Father, why don't you say a few words?"

It was all he needed. Before anyone realized he was confronting the audience, his hand uplifted—his voice happy—"My friends"— they looked up and beheld him beaming upon

[22]

them through the shadows, "I have just been asked to say a few words"—and for thirty or more minutes he told them of the Abandoned Christ Who hung limp, and taut, and dried, upon a tree that would bring forth the Fruit of Life.

His confreres testify to his power to sway audiences of both men and women. He was always ready and willing to talk and often would talk twice the time he was allotted. He could persuade in private conversation, too, by the sheer force of his trust in God and his understanding of the human heart in relation to God's Mercy. And because of this he was called upon time and time again to do a much needed missionary work dear to the heart of all priests, a work which Father Judge has committed to his spiritual sons.

About 1905 his zeal flared white, like magnesium, and the dazzling light of his love for God plunged him irrevocably into a series of good works that led him through a labyrinth of persecutions and triumphs, weariness of body, and the loneliness of misunderstanding.

First, it was the Holy Name. Everywhere on the missions he preached the Holy Name. His intensity for corralling members for the Holy Name Society throughout the country made him neglect other things seemingly more necessary for the missions. Every man who went to confession to him who was unwilling to join the Holy Name Society was in for a good long argument, no matter how many men or hundreds of men were waiting to be heard. Years later we see the result of his love of the Holy Name.

On the feast of the Holy Name, January 2, 1925, the Missionary Servants of the Most Blessed Trinity took over the administration of the General Hospital in Gadsden, Alabama, and the name was changed to the Holy Name of Jesus Hospital. "Think," said Father Judge to his children, "how many thousands of people will be taught to love the Holy Name of Jesus. Think of the thousands of letters that will go out all over the world,

Father Judge at Ordination

and the letters that will come back with the Holy Name of Jesus on the outside." When he spoke like this, all who heard him could not help but feel that the Holy Spirit hovered directly over this man. He had a way that made people do whatever he wished. He brushed aside all formal difficulties and went directly to the point.

In 1907 he worked just as zealously to gain members to the Archconfraternity of the Holy Agony. Everyone who came to his missions must belong to this Society. He would start a sermon perhaps upon Socialism, which at that time was beginning to be noticed as a menace to the faith of many Catholics of the Eastern states, but in the midst of his discourse he would be liable to switch to the tragedy of the Crucifixion.

"Poor dead Christ," he would say, "the present way of living is a long way from You, and You are a long way from it. Current events in up-to-date society haven't much use for the wounds of Jesus

[25]

Christ. The less we think of the wounds of Jesus the more we must wound another, and the more we think of His wounds the less we wound each other. How antiquated Your holy Gospel is becoming, and yet it is the only Gospel. It is what the world needs—meditation on the wounds of our Blessed Saviour. Let us keep near those wounds. You are safe from worldly lives, as long as you think of the wounds of Jesus. As long as they have a compassionate thought in your mind, the devil won't be able to lead you astray."

About this time, too, he began to form a movement, within the Lay Apostolate, among Catholic young women for the purpose of gaining careless Catholic girls or girls living under dangerous conditions back to the Sacraments. No one saw then that this would lead to the founding of two Religious Communities. No one saw then that his other "specializations" were simply his training under God for the life-work that has endeared him to hundreds of thousands, and has saved unnumbered souls, and will still save them.

He labored at this with the same intensity that characterized all his works. And he used the same methods. He worked tirelessly and sleeplessly. He went from place to place giving missions and gathering more members. His correspondence increased daily. He would be in his room until one in the morning writing letters.

He would be in the confessional at five o'clock in the morning; and from half past one until three o'clock in the afternoon when others would be resting, he would be out organizing his "associates" in Manhattan or Brooklyn and hurrying to get back to the confessional for the three o'clock session. "He worked harder at the mission than any of us," writes one of his companions of the mission, "and besides, outside of the mission work, did work that was far more exhausting—and all with but four hours' sleep at night. I just knew he couldn't

[27]

last—but he did. He was dreadfully in earnest."

With the young missioner it was always the same.

"Child, how much do you love God?" he would ask a boy, a girl, or a man or woman; and upon receiving an encouraging answer he would tell them of the great good they could do and encourage them not to be fearful, that God would reward their humble courage. "It would be too bad," he said, "because of a slight emotion of timidity, to omit a great good, or to do ourselves a little violence for God's honor for the small price of doing something a little unpleasant."

He loved his own with the love of a Father and he selected them for their genuineness and their willingness to give themselves entirely to the service of God and his poor. The ungenerous soul was discarded. The secret of his success may be found in this: That he insisted that all of his spiritual children should sanctify themselves. "Let your conversation be in Heaven."

In all of his undertakings, prayer was the power behind the movement. "Prayer will give you power over the demons and render you victorious in every temptation." "The prayerful spirit sees God in everything, hears His Will in the wind, and sees Him on the city streets." "The Will of God is learned in prayer. There we become courageous."

It is not that he simply preached prayer, he prayed himself. He was tireless in prayer. When he started to pray you could never be certain when he would stop. Just when you might begin to feel that he had finished his conversation with Heaven, he would recall some Saint to whom he had not paid respects. And when fatigue would overcome his children he would be liable to ask you, "I wonder do we pray enough," or, "Hold on to your rosary, we have to keep that moving because we need all kinds of things."

[29]

The car could not start until prayers had been said. The rosary must be recited on the way to town. What better conversation than with her who is the Queen of the Cenacle, the Mother of Light? Before he would talk with you, you would be asked to pray with him. It is told that once while riding on a train he offended another because in the very middle of a conversation he stopped his friend and asked him to say the rosary. This might be rudeness in another, but not with Father Judge. His mind was constantly on the things of God. How could he help the sweet breeze of the Dove of Peace that forever pressed against his ears?

Again, his confreres give testimony of his devotion to prayer, and his exactitude in the observance of the rule. Hear them: "He was a model Religious." "He was the most intense Novice I ever was acquainted with." "He was easily the best Religious of his time." "He loved to talk religious subjects with those who were interested, but this made him a little unpopular for we felt that we had directors for such purposes." Ah, but how could human eyes discern the burning heart of this young Novice, the love of God making his every day and night an everlasting prayer? Another says, "One morning when I had been absent from the conclusion of morning prayers, he came to my desk with a prayer book inviting me to make sure that I had not forgotten to say the Litany of the Holy Name." The Holy Name of Jesus! Jesu! It was ever the same until the very day of his death, "Jesus knows—He understands."

He seemed to live continually in the awareness of the Presence of God. No one could carry on a conversation with him without having it lead back to God, His Church or His Saints. He never pedantically intruded religion, but his mind was so much concerned with the things of God that he could not but speak of them. There was nothing of the Puritan in his attitude. He was pious, indeed, but he could also discuss current topics as well as religious matters, being well versed in the affairs of the day.

But the fever began to rise in the blood of Father Judge. The fever that filled the veins of the Apostles on the first Pentecost. We see him in these years in Manhattan and Brooklyn and Connecticut and New Jersey, gathering the children, instructing them himself or turning them over to his devoted workers, whose numbers increased daily. We see him follow in the footsteps of Saint Vincent, a father to the poor. How true are the words of *The Vincentian* in recording his death, "The poor have lost a friend."

We see him in the Bowery talking and preaching to every class of unfortunate humanity.

How grieved he would be after an excursion into these slums of pitiable living, exhausted and worn out, sorrowful that the Divine precept, "Whose sins you shall forgive they are forgiven them," was so difficult to fulfill amid

[32]

the crowded peoples who called the Bowery home.

And the children there in the Bowery, laughing children, who did not know that the Sweetest Child of all children might teach them games that are born in Heaven.

"The heart of the Cenacle must bleed for them," he says sadly. "These children belong to those who seek the Abandoned work, the Abandoned place, the Abandoned soul. They are yours in God. Consider for a moment the Divine Infant Jesus. Look at Him on the breast of His Immaculate Mother Mary or gaze upon Him in the arms of Saint Joseph—the Child Jesus. Why did He become a child? Why did He take this condition of helplessness? We know it was to protect the child. It was to extol the child. It was that He might become an advocate for the rights of the child. 'Suffer the little children to come unto me' (Mark 10, 14). An opportunity is given to us that is comparable to a destiny, to cherish

[33]

these children. Plead with the Triune
God for them."

And again,

"You are called upon to do things I
cannot do as a priest. If I cannot do
them and you will not do them, what is to
become of these children? Remember the
Good Shepherd. He went out after
them."

And over and over again,

"I never can pray any greater blessing
than for you to teach some child about the
Trinity. Greater and more wonderful is
the act of him who traces this Cross upon
a little child and teaches its use, than he
who takes a kingdom with many battles,
for in one instance the conqueror had a
triumph that will last but a few days, in
the other there has been a victory of faith
that will be celebrated for all eternity,
with the exalted Cross of Jesus in Para-
dise."

[34]

About 1909 Father Judge was removed from the missionary band and changed to parish work in Saint John's, Brooklyn. It is easy to understand that his heart was sorely tried by this change, but he took it heroically. Complaints were made that he was using the missions simply to gain recruits for his associations. His confreres were nettled not so much by what he did, as by what he did not do. They could not fathom the reason for it all. But who can understand a man of God? Who could understand that the Holy Ghost was pushing him on, guiding him? Who could understand the desolation of his heart when he saw the thousands and thousands that were being lost to the Faith?

Christ Himself was terribly misunderstood even by those whom He had trained. Nor could He please everyone. And so Father Judge let the sweet Providence of God guide him. The movement spread as he moved about. It sprang up wherever he gave a mission. He could not help himself. He believed sincerely that God wished him to do this work. He had no assurance of what it would lead to or where it would end. When complaints reached him he paid no attention to them. "Let no man interfere with a vocation," he said, "or with God's work." He studied the Scriptures and told his helpers that the second Epistle of Saint Paul to the Corinthians was a particular message for them. "I call your attention especially to the sixth chapter, the fourth verse and on: 'But in all things let us exhibit ourselves as the ministers of God, in much patience, in tribulation, in necessities, in distress . . . in sweetness, in the Holy Ghost, in charity unfeigned.' "

About 1910 he was changed again, to Saint Vincent's Mission in Springfield, Massachusetts. The work followed him, and grew. Since he could not be with the various groups in as many cities, he kept constantly in touch with them by means of letters, and by messages through other associates.

[36]

"This is your vocation," he said, "to do Jesus Christ a personal service. It is your vocation to go amidst horrible conditions, abandoned conditions, impossible conditions, to do something for the image of the Blessed Trinity, threatening perils for the sake of a soul. There was the crucifying; it opened those wounds so large. They left nothing undone. Not a drop was left in the Body."

The good works performed by these devoted followers increased and multiplied. Hundreds of children were gathered in city streets and country lanes, wherever a place was accessible, and taught the truths of their religion; children, who for many reasons, might never otherwise have learned there was a God; babies and grown children, too, were brought to the baptismal font; hardened sinners to the confessional and parents to the Church where their marriages were validated and their homes preserved.

How pleased he was when he heard of their

progress and labors. He drove them on by
the very force of his own goodness. They
must not lag behind, or slow up. Theirs is a
mission that admits no tepidity.

"I intended to get all I could out of
you for Christ and His Church," he tells
them on retreat. "I came with that de-
liberate purpose—to develop your life so
that the Church could get much out of
you. The battles of the Church are
fought outside—in the house, and in the
workshop. All good movements have a
care for the Christian laity strengthened
by the priests. The Saints have done
work for the Church; you are the successors of these. Your lives are to be so
high, so pure, so unpolluted, so virtuous
that they will be an invincible argument
for the Church of Christ."

Again, we ask, who could understand him?
He could not understand himself. "God's
Will be done." Over and over again he re-
peated it. His critics grew more apprehen-

sive as men and women joined the movement. "A saint or a fool," says one. "A fanatic," said another. "A Martin Luther," spoke a third. "A visionary," said a fourth. To all Father Judge replied, "God's Will be done."

In 1913 a Missionary Cenacle was opened on Madison Street, Baltimore, Maryland. In 1915 a Cenacle was opened in an Italian quarter at Orange, New Jersey. Whenever it was possible the director visited these workers and consulted with them. But when he was not there in person his letters came regularly, filled with hope and encouragement, and good cheer, and prayers that the Holy Ghost would guide them.

And just when it seemed that the work had become firmly rooted, a "catastrophe" happened that seemed to his zealous workers the end of their hopes and plans. Father Judge was transferred from Springfield, Massachusetts, to Opelika, Alabama. The work was ended. Their director was going miles and miles away. To many, Alabama was no nearer

[39]

than South Africa. They began a novena at that time that the change would not material- ize. Father Judge stopped it. *"If it is of God,"* he said once more, *"the work will go on. If it is not, let it perish immediately."* And so he asked all the good men and women who had been helping him, to further assist him in his preparation for this new crusade. He had them make crosses from little twigs so that he could plant them in this cross-less country where the tragedy of Good Friday caused lit- tle feeling. He brought with him hundreds of Miraculous Medals and scattered them over this land where the name of Mary was no more than a name.

On August 10, 1915, the feast of Saint Lawrence, he said Mass in the Missionary Cenacle at Orange, New Jersey. Again he spoke to his sorrowing children of the Provi- dence of God. "Be peaceful," he said to them. "Be sure to get to confession every week. Do not omit your rosary. How sweet are the ways of Divine Providence." And then with

HOLY TRINITY SHRINE

fatherly simplicity he would add, "Pray for your Father, my dear children, pray that he may do great things for God. Work up your devotion to Saint Joseph, be patient and he will aid you." And with a blessing he was gone. He left for Alabama, with this one thought only in his mind, "God's Will be done."

But you could not stop Father Judge. Timidity was never one of his failings. Rather, resourcefulness was one of his shining qualities. He saw in a flash that here was a marvelous field for the Lay Apostolate. Here again he met children, thousands of children without any knowledge of God, or of His Mother. He called upon his volunteers in the North to help him. And who will tell the story of those first few workers who gave up everything that this life could offer to go South into a strange land.

There was no idea of Religious Communities at that time. The women who went down were "ladies," and the men were "men."

Father Judge had nothing in mind other than that they would help him. Writing sometime later in *The Ecclesiastical Review,* he states:

"We priests could do little to break down these gigantic walls of prejudice and misrepresentations. Sisters, too, are powerless, because they are under suspicion. What is to be done? The Fathers did everything, published a magazine, held non-Catholic missions, carried on many charities and were priestly in their lives. Inspiration and plan were sought from the Holy Ghost in prayer and counsel as to necessary action. He graciously made manifest the means to counteract this vexatious opposition.

"There was, because of the fewness of our number, one thing yet untried, and this force that has been a tremendous evangelizing power since the day of Our Lord Himself—the *highly spiritualized laity;* in other words, the Lay Apostolate. To demonstrate Catholicity through them as a merchant does his goods was the principle evoked. The invincible argument

[42]

against slander was the open lives of a
number of refined, enlightened and virtuous Catholic men and women. Frequent
contact with them on the part of the na-
tives, daily association and much ques-
tioning about their faith and practice,
have accomplished results that seemed
beyond the efforts of our priests. When
every other means failed, the Fathers ap-
pealed to edifying and self-sacrificing
daughters of the Holy Mother Church to
make common cause with them in the in-
terests of Religion."

And they answered so generously that even
Father Judge himself must have been surprised. What did he have to offer them in the
Southland to which he called them? Did he
give any thought to the matter? Did he just
ask these men and women to come South without any reflection as to the hardships they were
about to face and the trials that they must
endure?

These men and women were not deceived in
coming South as to the life they would live.

Father Judge was always open and above board. Always when a question arose he would say to his children, "Give me three reasons for, and three reasons against." And then he would weigh one against the other, while asking the Holy Spirit for Light. Let us quote from a letter which he sent to one of the early groups who offered their services.

"I have weighed the matter discussed, and have confided it to the Holy Ghost; and the first three reasons I thought of pointing to the Will of God were these:

"(1) Contact with Southerners. This is most essential for Church progress. God will do much through you and your friends that we priests cannot accomplish, not only to win recalcitrant Catholics back, but to make non-Catholics more enlightened and more tolerant of Catholics. God will use you to prepare the way for our ministry.

"(2) You will help the Catholic movement of colonizing and Catholicizing the South. Bishops and priests have been

[44]

sad and discouraged because of the seem-
ing hopelessness of efforts to evangelize
and convert the South, even to get a foot-
ing for the Church. Thank God that He
is using the Missionary Cenacle, the name
given to our people and their work, to
show that it is possible to drive a wedge
into such conditions. You and the others
will be as it were so many sledge hammers
to drive the wedge in further.

"(3) Above all, the splendid field to
operate the spiritual and corporal works
of mercy. How much glory will be given
to God and good done to the souls and
bodies of our neighbors; edification will
be given and God will use you generous
young men as the foundation of a new
Catholicity in a country where there is
most powerful conspiracy of agencies of
evil and error and worldliness and heresy
and the devil to destroy our Holy Faith
and to keep the Church out. The word
of Saint Paul to the Romans 11, 5, 'The
just judgment of God, Who will render
to every man according to his works. To
them, indeed, who according to patience

in good work, seek glory and honor and incorruption, eternal life. . . . But glory and honor and peace to every one that worketh good.' May these promised blessings be realized in all of you and that you may earn by your zeal and perseverance the other pledged reward of the Holy Ghost: 'If a man be a server of God, and doth His Will, him He heareth' (John 9, 31).

"Against these reasons for your coming I diligently also thought what might be against it. There are three possible objections.

"(1) Inconstancy. Young men may be fired with generous impulses but when put to a test they lack stamina, they do not love God enough to sacrifice; they wish to serve God, not so much His way as their way; therefore, when they are contradicted, corrected, disappointed, when their self-pride and love are hurt, they complain and murmur, become discontented and spread this contagion. All of you, however, have been waiting so long, you have been severely tried, and in

[46]

spite of disappointment just heaped upon disappointment, you have persevered; so this first reason is much canceled.

"(2) There is a condition of bigotry and unfriendliness against the Church. This means for you insult will be heaped upon insult and wrong upon wrong and unless you can rejoice in suffering for Him Who suffered for us and be patient and prayerful under trial, you will quickly surrender to discouragement. Then, too, you will feel the lack of many comforts and the pinch of necessity.

"(3) You will be associated with others who have labored as apostles in the very worst of these conditions. You and they, indeed, have much in common, a great love of God, a zealous desire to do much for His honor and glory and the salvation of souls, but you will be under their rule and guidance as superiors, directed of course by the Priest. Can you develop and show this humility and obedience; can you for the love of God and to help save souls forget yourselves this much?

[47]

"Study all for and against; study prayerfully the reasons for your not coming; if they disappear, or if they at least reduce themselves to mere repugnance, or to a fear, or to mere doubt, then in God's Holy Name, Come! Come to give honor and glory and adoration to God the Father and God the Son and God the Holy Ghost. Come and help the Church. Come and build up an empire for Jesus Christ, come and be a comfort for His dear sake to those sick in body and soul. You will be obliged to begin from the ground up. This is good for it is the way of all God's works. Their foundations must be laid in prayer, in labor, in trial, in sacrifice, and the more of these the more of God in them, and therefore the more of success and immortality."

Could ever an appeal be more tenderly beautiful? Consider the yearning, burning heart of Father Judge. He saw this magnificent field ready for the harvest, but without harvesters. He felt the sweet impulses of the Holy Ghost urging him to call for volunteers from the North. Humanly, he knew it was a tremendous sacrifice to ask of them. He remembered he had been called a fool. Was this proof of his folly?

Consider now, the immense joy that flooded his soul when volunteers came forward. He asked something because he felt God wished him to ask it—and his generous-hearted friends in the North threw themselves with utter abandonment into the arms of Divine Providence under the direction of this pioneer-priest. It was truly a hundredfold reward for this humble son of Saint Vincent. He could not reward them; he could not hide the difficulties they were to face; so he left all to God and told his new helpers,

"Martyrdom may not be our grace, but many of us are called to suffer the less brilliant but perhaps even more meritorious martyrdom of life, 'With its longer agony and its constant sting of petty annoyances, of cruel spite, contempt and calumny.' "

[49]

Undaunted, they persevered. Their modesty, charity, meekness and Christian refinement caused sentiment to turn gradually in their favor. During that time many an insult, patiently suffered, they offered Him Who for them suffered so much. God was touched by their constancy and He realized in their favor the words of the Psalmist, "Trust in the Lord, and do good, and dwell in the land, and thou shalt be fed with its riches" (Ps. 36, 3). Years later Father Judge remarked, "The most glorious chapters of Religious Communities are the chapters made by the missionaries who went to places where there was seemingly no hope."

As it was with Saint Vincent de Paul, of the two groups Father Judge formed, the one for men and the other for women, the latter was the larger. We cannot fail to notice a close parallel. Saint Vincent de Paul called upon many priests to help, but it is said that in the beginning, of the few followers he had, only one declared himself ready to begin actively in the evangelization of the peasants of France. Two men for the whole of France! After ten years there were but thirty-five. And Father Judge started off with two men in his work in the South.

Saint Vincent de Paul interested many women in his work. The first Daughters of Charity were not, strictly speaking, members of a Religious Order. They sought the poor, their cloister was the street and as Saint Vincent told them endlessly, "Let your office and your litany be the poor; they will suffice. In their service put all else aside. In doing this you leave God only to find Him. The poor alone demand your time. Treat them well, with gentleness, with tenderness, with love, for they are your lords and masters, and mine. They are the nobility of heaven. It is they who will open the gates of heaven." Saint Louise de Marillac was the first superior of these daughters, and upon her Saint Vincent placed the heavy responsibility of being a mother to them. Her death preceded his own by a few months.

Father Judge, likewise, had more women interested in the movement than men. They came from all classes, with only one thought, to help do good. When their numbers grew so that they needed a Mother to guide them, he called upon the Holy Ghost, and after much prayer appointed Lulu Keasey, a young country school teacher from the hills of western Pennsylvania, who came and brought with her the charms of calm simplicity, a tender love of God, and a generous, willing heart.

As Mother Boniface she was destined to shine like the Christmas Star over this little Bethlehem in Alabama. Her zeal for the things of God will ever be remembered by those who love and revere her name. Mother Boniface Keasey understood Father Judge. She knew him perhaps as well as anyone of those who were intimately associated with him. And he leaned heavily upon her. She tried to anticipate his wishes. She made his burdens lighter. She had a tender mother love that embraced not only the work and the workers, but the entire field of action, the Church— God! One could never meet her without being immediately captured by her smile. Countless numbers of men and women went to her for advice. She was known afar for charity and kindness. She was the consolation of hundreds of priests. She it was, who helped lead the Sisters through those first stages of suffering. She it was who stood close to Father Judge as he held in his hands "the Precious Burden" and watched the Sister's motherhouse, a labor of fifteen years, be reduced to ashes in two hours.

After this terrible calamity she writes, at the end of a letter to her children describing the fire, "It just seems too terrible to be true. We are back to where we were fifteen years ago. We will start all over again with a big debt, but God's Holy Will be done. 'The Lord gave, and the Lord hath taken away; blessed be the name of the Lord' (Job 1, 21).

We know it is all for the best. We only want to know His Will, and as best we can we will carry it out. God love and bless all of you."

She died in the performance of duty on November 22, 1931.

The shock to Father Judge can only be imagined. He had depended upon this wise and strong woman of God. To see her snatched from him would certainly have crushed a less spiritualized character. On the night of her death he wrote a Cenacle letter to her sorrowing children and friends. It is an exquisite eulogy written in deep sorrow. But he did not show his sorrow. Instead, he reminded those who folded and helped him send these letters out to the Missionary Cenacles that they were not to forget to cross them in the Name of the Triune God. *That* was important.

While Mother Boniface's body lay in the chapel close by, the one who had appointed her Mother wrote,

"Dying, she said she was not afraid to die. How like our Mother, the good, the

strong, the wise woman of God. We have
only known kindness in her and seen
goodness; the fruits of her life are surely
beautiful. How precious now are the
works of her charity and those number-
less deeds of mercy, corporal and spiritual. What a reward she will have for
the souls she has helped, the children she
has aided, the young girls she has at-
tracted to God, the young men whom
she has helped along the way to the holy
priesthood. What a comforter she has
been to all who came within the sweet
attraction of her life; what a service she
has ever rendered to Church and religion,
and what an untiring and generous service
this has been. 'Veni Sponsa Mea.' She
heard the summons and answered it but it
does not mean that she has left us. We
have the consoling doctrine of the Communion of Saints for our consolation. Let
us remember her now who never forgot us
in life. We, her children, can see no im-
perfections in our Mother, but God is to
be the Judge. Lest there be aught to be
satisfied to His Eternal Justice and In-

finite Sanctity, do not forget her soul. Remember her in prayer over the days that are to come for after all it is only the Church who can say, 'Sancta.' "

This is the Lord's doing (*Ps. 117, 23*)

CHAPTER TWO

THE work went on, and spread into many dioceses and into Puerto Rico. The Isle of Enchantment fascinated him. His daughters were there in 1923, his sons followed in 1926. They faced difficult conditions. Father Judge could not be with them always, but he visited them as often as he could. He loved the Island because of its poverty, but mostly because of its children.

"We must form Catholic leaders," he said, "and these boys must bring from Saint Augustine's to their homes a fine type of Catholicity. . . . This, it seems to me, is the secret of the reconstruction of Catholic Life in the Spanish-American world and the only real worthwhile remedy for Mexican troubles or any kind of misery; in other words, given that it is possible to cleanse the root, to Catholicize, to spiritualize the boy, what a foundation will be had for any movement of reformation or reconstruction."

Four foundations of his communities, three of Sisters, and one of Priests and Brothers have been established on the Island; two of these in schools, one a place of residence for young women students of the University of Puerto Rico, and one a missionary center for work among the poor, and the children.

A house of study was opened at the Catholic University for the students. Vocations poured in and the man of God found himself the center of tremendous responsibilities that grew into greater proportion than anyone could have possibly foreseen. Money shortages arose, but that did not deter him. Most religious movements have been started on nothing and have been supported from scanty and irregular revenues. He took journeys whenever he thought his presence was needed. When he found an abandoned

[60]

mission he searched for more missionaries to take care of it.

One of his sons called over long distance and said to him, "Father, it is an urgent difficulty. What shall we do?" Over the wire came the reply, "Can you meet me in Atlanta tomorrow morning at five o'clock?" And he traveled over a thousand miles to come to the aid of his missionaries in the South.

"Father, we have no money to take care of this bill." "Have you told Saint Joseph," he would reply, and when you answered, "Yes," he would say to you, "Go back and tell him again." He would empty his pockets and give you perhaps sixty-eight cents, or maybe a little more than a dollar. "I do not want you to get rich," he said, "for that would worry me a whole lot. If we do not have some annoyances, where would we have the opportunity for practicing patience and the other virtues."

One Christmas Eve he learned of a family who would like to hear Mass the next morning. Where did they live? He wasn't sure. It was in the general direction of Alabama and Georgia. No, he was not certain of the name. Get them and bring them to church. Where will they stay after the Mass? "That's God's business. Now run along, and the Lord bless you." Dark roads, bumpy, dusty roads, miles and miles out into nowhere, roads that led to a shanty, with an oil lamp, and a single table, and an open fire, and four beds, one in each corner; a mother and a father—and eight children. As many as could be transported heard Mass on Christmas.

Constantly, with greater energy as the days passed, he planned his crusade for souls. Tell him a novel idea and he would work it to do some spiritual good. "We are having a contest here," he writes from Puerto Rico, "a Ten Commandment Contest. Prizes will be given to those giving the best answers to the questions, What are the Ten Commandments? and, What are the best ways to make people think of them?"

From the same Island he sends this thought,

"You have in the States drives for money, drives for this affair or that, but did you ever hear of a drive for Baptisms?"

Riding horseback through the hills of Puerto Rico, seeking the poor and those who needed help, brought him memories of another ride. "I thought of the Blessed Mother going into the hill country of Judea. I suppose she had these riding experiences."

To him a day was not just a nice day—it was a wonderful day, a glorious day, a magnificent day. Only God could make a lovely day. Whatever God did was grand. A day was truly a marvelous thing to create. And the heart of Father Judge forever kept thumping a joyous *Benedicite*. "Gratitude implies appreciation," he said. "It insists upon the realization of how and whence favors have come, and recognition by some external response should be made to show the interior sentiments that we have of thankfulness."

He preached frequent Communion long before the idea became popular. He was openly and severely criticized. Years later we find he was right. "I fell back on first principles," he told his children. "I always tried to be right with the Church. I got this from the history of the Church and the Fathers. Secondly, I followed the principle, 'By their fruits you shall know them.' Are the Fathers' fruits good? I studied. One day I found in Saint Augustine: 'We should so live that every time we go to Mass we may receive Communion.' That settled me. I had Saint Augustine back of me."

And so with the most childlike familiarity he would explain the various reasons why you should receive frequently. To those who would be seen very seldom at the Communion rail he might say, "Why, when Our Lord does come to you, maybe for your Easter duty, He will say to you, 'Why, hello! I hardly knew you!'" Irreverent? Rather, it shows a mind tuned to the things of God to such a point that he really considered Christ his elder brother. God does not like distance either in saint or sinner. John

[64]

laid his head upon the Master's breast. Mary Magdalen wiped His feet with her hair.

He rejoiced in the good fortune that came to others, especially to those in the service of the King of Kings. If he considered himself at all it was as the least of the King's servants. On being reminded of the ordination of a large group of men for another community he writes to the superior: "How consoled you must be in the ordination of such a large band. May the Triune God be praised for bestowing so many vocations on your Community and may this blessing remain with you long."

He was proud of his God and would tell you of Him like the little boy who says his father is the biggest and best man of all men. The magnificence of God appalled him. God made the sun and the moon, and all the colors of the sky. And Father Judge could never look upon these wonders of the Omnipotent without telling you of it. "I am thinking of a glorious sunset I saw in the Berkshire hills. A glorious ending to a glorious day, rose red through the sky. The first thought of a prayerful soul would be: 'Praise to God Who created it.' The second would be to thank Him. It is an exhilaration to me to think that this is the God I serve. How glorious this sunset! How glorious will be my setting, my death! Only the memory of good done will be there to make us happy at death."

He loved coincidences that reminded him of God and holy things. He loved all the simple joys of life, a budding tree, a raindrop, a sugar-cane festival, a bloom of cotton for its purity, and a stalk of corn for its majesty. He liked sports and music. All of his classmates speak of the beauty of his tenor voice. But he did not like ceremony, or to be the center of attraction. "High estimation," he said, "is at times embarrassing because it holds one so painfully to high ideals or rather unreasonable ideals."

His ideal was simplicity. He liked good food and farms. The story of his love of farms is for another day; it is alive with all the glory of God's creation. He loved games and children's plays. The smile of a child could distract him from the most exacting work. And through all of his days, whether in joy or sorrow, in want or plenty, he poured forth a symphony of Faith and Hope, Charity and Peace.

FAITH—HOPE

The just man liveth by faith (*Romans, 1, 17*)
I will put my trust in him (*Hebrews, 2, 13*)

CHAPTER THREE

Who can describe the beauty of Father Judge's faith? The artist's canvas is not large enough, nor are words equal to it. You would have to see the light that flashed in his eyes, and the laughter that pursed his lips; you would have to watch him pause a moment, and lower his head toward his heart as though an inner Voice were sending a message through the corridors of his soul.

You would have to be there then to catch the throbbing cadences of his husky voice as he poured forth his overwhelming trust and confidence and love of the Father, and the Son, and the Holy Ghost. His faith was everywhere. It was beautiful, and it was childlike. It fell across the years like slanting sunlight and in the darkest hours it shone the brightest.

"The Lord is with us," he would say. "He is in the boat. There may be any kind of tempest about, but Jesus is with us. Have confidence and courage then, that first of all will save us from the reproach, 'Ye of little faith.' Secondly, that will bring upon us His joy and blessing and praise, 'Such faith I have not found in Israel.' "

All cries of hope and misery and despair found a sympathetic echo in his heart, but he never wavered.

"There is one advantage of necessity," he writes, "there is one joy to be found in biting need, there is consolation even when the darkest clouds overshadow. It is this: we have an opportunity of registering a supreme act of trust and confidence in a Being, supremely and infinitely good and loving. It is not so much that we do a thing or get a thing or have a thing, or have a prayer answered, but that we show an invincible faith and courage in Jesus Christ. Supposing we can get a

[72]

faith like that. Even suppose the whole
fabric of everything should be thrown
down, what soothing to one's conscience
to say: I have not failed in faith or trust
in God. If, therefore, a current jamming
and pressure of events furnish us opportunity to qualify for such high graces, we
should feel a present joy in what to many
might mean fear, and anxiety, and even
despondency. The loving Providence of
God takes note of the burnt blade of grass
in the field and the passing of the animal
in the bush and the fluttering of the small-
est resident of the birdland."

"Oh, that majestic formula of Faith,"
he cried, "the Apostles' Creed."

When questioned concerning the acquisi-
tion of this virtue he would look at you as if
you should know this.

"Such power comes from the stinging
experience of need when we are thrown
back on Divine Providence."

And again when faith seemed to have been
misplaced,

"This virtue flourished not so much on the top of Mount Thabor as in the Garden of Gethsemane, and at the foot of the pillar of flagellation and the cross of Calvary."

The January before his death he wrote:

"What matter the tempest outside when God is ruling sweetly and benignly inside. We just think of the Ark, and of the Cenacle that first Holy Thursday night."

When it seemed as though a mistake had been made, his faith was ready.

"Divine Providence will not permit us to be very wrong or to make any mistake except that which will revert to His honor and glory and serve our own cause better. Think of the faith of Saint Joseph. Saint Joseph had desperate anxieties."

And then he would relate the sorrow Saint Joseph felt before Jesus was born. How

[74]

could he know or understand or realize how it came about that his Mary was to become a mother? The evidence was so overwhelming and he loved her so tenderly. But he could not fathom the dreamings of her blue eyes or the beauty of her radiant charm. And he would tell you how in time the angel told Saint Joseph not to fear, that the burden Mary carried within her womb was the incalculable weight of Divinity.

That the secret of her eyes, the glow of her face, the charm of her step, the gracefulness of her manner were reflections not only of her Immaculate Conception, but of the miracle of the Word Made Flesh. How that must have stunned him! His watchfulness and care and anxiety increased as the time neared for the birth of Jesus. No one could be poorer than Saint Joseph was on that first Christmas night. This was a Royal Child and he wanted Him to have a royal birth. He wanted Him to have royal clothes, and friends there to

[75]

help Mary in her need. Instead, the Child was born in a stable and wrapped in common swaddling clothes. And Mary was alone when the little Jesus was born.

But was Father Judge's faith imprudent, overconfident, or unaware of the terrific responsibilities and destitute situations? Rather the direct opposite. Why, his faith in God was all he had! Accordingly he wrote to the Vincentian Father who was his immediate superior:

"The Mission was extremely desolate, conditions apparently hopeless, and the progress seen here today, through God's help, came of an attempt to do the work that was set before me and to provide the proper agents for carrying it on. What has been affected was done not so much by any preconceived plan for the future but rather to provide workers and maintenance for the daily problem. God in His own Providence has sent the workers and the means to maintain them."

What did he think of himself and his workers?

"At best we are nothing but poor frontiersmen of the Church leading that kind of a life in the hope that we can be of service in isolated places and reach souls that otherwise would be lost to the regular ministrations of the clergy."

And a little farther on in the same letter,

"Let me again reiterate, if the Church wishes us to go on, we want to go on; if the Church does not wish us to go on, we do not want to go on, therefore, let it be as the Church wishes."

"We are still in the shallows and often enough hear the grating and grinding of our boat. There is always some obstruction to keep us prayerful and hopeful in Divine Providence."

Often he compared the Missionary Cenacle to a ship:

[77]

"The ship of the Missionary Cenacle must of course expect many head winds and tempestuous disturbances."

And very simply he would tell you:

"We are just a baby Community and are praying and hoping that the Triune God may be pleased to make use of us."

But where did his support come from? What kept him going?

"Everything is a gift of God, every breath we breathe, every step we take, every heart beat, every coursing blood-drop, all our seeing, and hearing, the food we eat, all that we possess, all that we can sense and visibly perceive are gifts of the Holy Ghost in the natural order."

Did he take too much upon himself? Did he have too many irons in the fire for so young a Community? Why bother with the Puerto Rican work until affairs were more settled?

"The Apostolic spirit means exhaust of self. We have been obliged to expand rapidly, work has been pushed upon us. The Holy Ghost has sent us many and good vocations. It is our spirit to wish to work particularly in neglected places for an abandoned cause. 'Preservation of the Faith' is our watchword. You can understand therefore why we feel at home in Puerto Rico."

It is too bad to hold up the students. They should be pushed through, especially when priests are needed. Ah, but part of the student's training requires him to work on the missions before his ordination. He is a missionary. One of the Missionary Cenacle virtues is self-sacrifice. And besides Father Judge cautions his students:

"Remember you are always to be a missionary. Let your joy be in this even more than in being a student. The prayer of my heart for you is that you all be proficient in the science of the Saints, and

[79]

that the lesson that comes when we behold King Christ, will grow and grow upon you."

He encouraged his young men to be zealous in study but warned again and again lest ambition for knowledge crowd out prayer.

"Remember," he would say, "you are first and last missionaries. You are to be men of prayer—then students. Remember what I have told you so frequently before, that whatever induces to a spirit of study and piety is a blessing of the highest order. It follows therefore that those who promote such a spirit are God's angels in disguise. The spirit of study certainly is amongst you. . . . It is necessary that we have learned priests, but remember the Apostolic spirit is far more precious than any degree a University can offer. Want the degree, aspire to a degree, labor for the degree, with purity of intention for what the degree stands for, but over and above all this, pray and

[80]

work for those graces which are necessary
for a missionary."

The faith and perseverance of Father Judge
was constant. And after some new marvel of
Divine love had been made known to him as a
reward for his faith, like a child he would tell
you of it with eyes shining like skies after a
rain. His faith was as overwhelming as the
Mysteries he loved so dearly. And it is a
thought entrancing, to ponder what must be
his exquisite rapture now to behold the Mystery of the Incarnation revealed—the Ma-
ternity Incomprehensible—the Mother of the
Word Made Flesh, and the Beatific Vision!

. . . .

And how boundless was the hope of Father
Judge! "Did you ever hear of the man who
hoped against hope?" he would ask. "You'll
find him in Saint Paul's Epistle to the
Romans." And at another time when clouds
were heavy and thunder rumbled, and light-
ning seemed ready to strike with fury, he re-

marked, "I have confided my troubles to the
Little Flower of Jesus. I know she will not
fail us; so hope on. Hope on and on and on."
And again, "My son, there is a fundamental
virtue called hope, confidence in God, and
without some perfection in this virtue not one
of us is rightly fit as an instrument in God's
hands for some particular or special work in
which He wishes to use us. This virtue, however, cannot be developed by theory or by
merely reading books or listening to conferences on it. These acts flower only in distressful moments and emergencies and crises."

When he could not seemingly impart this
trust to another he might smile at you as if
you had completely overlooked the point, and
say with utter detachment and positive assurance, "Surely after standing thirty years at
the altar of the Triune God it is not presump-
tion to think that the Divine Majesty will take
note of the prayers of His poor priest."

Who could withstand such captivating simplicity and calm assurance? Tell him the ob-

stacle, show him all the known facts why such a thing was absolutely beyond the realm of reason, give him your figures, pour forth your best wisdom why he should desist, and he would listen attentively. But when you had finished, he would shake his head and burst forth with perfect conviction, "But" (and his arms would spread wide), "you do not allow for the Providence of God." As a great ecclesiastic said, "I was afraid to oppose him when he talked thus."

It was not that his hope was temperamental or varied or fair-weather hope. He breathed it; it enfolded him tenderly, like strong wings, and he was ever ready to inspire you with a desire to hope on and on and on.

CHARITY—PEACE

How beautiful are the feet of them that preach the gospel of peace (*Romans 10, 15*)

CHAPTER FOUR

I F the world is a garden, and charity the flower of virtues, then, wherever Father Judge went, he left behind him the delicate perfume of active charity, mental charity, and charity that bounded outside the boundaries of this finite world over the wall of Heaven and into the lap of the Good Shepherd Who long ago said that we must love one another. To everyone he said, "I behold you in God."

To try to praise his charity further would be to put a flashlight on the moon. The light of charity sparkled in his eyes. The music of charity made all his words a song. "For sweet charity's sake," he would say, and the most repulsive task or tedious journey or odious labor would be undertaken and accomplished by the all-embracing charity of his humble mind and priestly heart.

His messages and his conferences are founded on his method of "Bear and forbear; live and let live. Let each one of you constitute yourselves as a guardian of charity."

His letters thrill with the marvelous graces that come from an ever-increasing delight in this virtue. They gush from his heart as no other of his teachings. He despises a murmurer, a meddler, a whiner, but for the man who shows charity, ah, that man could have his very life.

"Where there is charity of speech, there is Heaven, and love of God and the love of neighbor flourishes like a palm tree. Outside of the harmony of the Celestial Host there is no symphony comparable to that where hearts and minds and wills and tongues are in accord. . . . Be vigilant. Be prudent. But, before all things, have charity."

He did not compute how much were the seventy times seven times that we should forgive our brother, but told you, "Charity al-

ways gives one more chance." He relished a
spirited debate at council and never ceased
asking your opinion of the particular subject
under discussion.

But always and always it was, "Be peaceful!
Want peace, work for peace. . . . Because
tranquil, the operation is peaceful, and because
peaceful it is of the Holy Ghost. It takes
the Holy Ghost to give such smoothness.
There is no lubrication like unto His Grace."
And then with a gesture convincing and com-
pelling, "Peace is the supreme achievement of
all human endeavor and striving."

Peace and always peace! Picture him on
the top step of the altar. His voice is vibrant
and fearless. A wave is threatening to swamp
the Missionary Cenacle bark. But he is not
afraid.

"Remember I have often warned you
that no harm can come to you except from
the inside. If we are united, the Evil
One rages in vain. Your work is of such
a nature that it is going to bring assaults

[89]

from the evil spirit. Let each one of you determine that he will keep the peace and that if adjustments are necessary they will be made in charity and obedience. That God's Will prevail, let each one determine that he will not be tenacious of his own will, and that if he will cherish any ambition, it will be to be a peacemaker and to obtain the promise that the Beatitude holds forth."

He deplored the harm that is done to good works by well-meaning but misguided people.

"The truth grows on me the longer I live, that more harm is done to the work of God, that there is more interference with good work, more confusion among His servants because of evil words spoken by good people than the harm that is effected by enemies against good works. . . . Peace is one of the fruits of the Holy Ghost. What a dreadful accounting that one must give who upsets and destroys it."

[90]

The charity of Father Judge was not confined to words. It always "gave another chance." It was exquisite in its simplicity, and simple in its operation. "Hospitality is a Christian virtue," he would remind you, and his house and his Missionary Cenacles and his arms were ever wide open to anyone who came, *In nomine Domini.* There was no damming the floods of his generous heart; his children could not keep pace with him.

And so it went on. Priests wrote him and asked if he would give another trial to a vocation who had perhaps had some difficulty elsewhere. And after inquiring and making sure that at least there was a proper amount of good heart and good will, he would reply, "The Providence of God, you never can tell how It will act. We must always depend on It and give It a chance to work."

Another time a letter reached him while he was in Puerto Rico, asking if he would accept a young man for the priesthood who, because of finances, could not be adopted elsewhere.

[91]

"Imagine," wrote Father Judge, "the impression your letter made upon me when I tell you that because of the immense loss of souls I am grieving very much because there are not six hundred priests on the island."

And again when some particular letter would manifest a natural human anxiety he would try to turn the thought to the anxieties of the Church. "There are several worries that I would like to give you that would make beautiful substitutes for those you have. One is this: What a shame it is that so little thought is given and so little love made manifest to the Mystery of the Holy Trinity, that foundation truth of our holy faith. It certainly can be said of our age that it is non-Trinitarian."

It was difficult at times for those who worked with him to become reconciled to his methods. His charity was so deep, so embracing and above the natural, that at times he might have seemed to be without the gift of common sense. And yet incidents like the

[92]

following won the most stubborn and obstinate of those who opposed him.

He had sent word to one of his Missions that they might expect another vocation who had volunteered to help the cause. He said the gentleman would be most willing and that he was thankful that he could come so soon. One of his spiritual sons wrote back to him immediately and pleaded with him to have pity on their poverty. How could they possibly take care of anyone else, especially one who was uncertain? He asked Father Judge to please defer the gentleman's coming. To this letter he replied in his tenderest manner. He acknowledged all the reasons why he should not take on a new vocation and showed a deep sympathy for the financial misery of the time. But he added:

"The Lord deliver us from the condition wherein everybody who comes within our portals must square with our conception of perfection. Brother dear, have you never heard the legends and stories from ancient days that would make us think perhaps sometimes in a poor wayfarer we may entertain an angel unawares? Again, dear Brother, packed away somewhere in the philosophy of charity of the Missionary Cenacle thought is this: for the sweet sake of the Lord and His Immaculate Mother there is always a place in the Missionary Cenacle Inn for him who comes to us *in nomine Domini.*"

And then in complete understanding he added:

"May the Gracious Queen of Heaven pity us in these plights into which we get for the cause of Her Divine Son."

When an adjustment had to be made or a reprimand given he was decisive and strict, but always he gave his corrections with a minimum of hurt by peace and charity and reverence.

Words cannot tell the story of this surpliced flower of God. The beauty of the bud was concealed in the manly vase. The full blooming, the richer fragrance, the finer appreciation was not meant for this finite world. Only in the shadow of the Mystical Rose could the petals open in the profusion of Heavenly Glory.

His big heart was wrapped up in the loveliness of the poor. And his pleasure was to be their humble servant. "I behold you in God," was perhaps his greatest expression of love for man. "I behold you in God"—and hope is born where despair had been, and love where before was hate, and peace where turmoil seethed, and Faith where strange gods had been pedestaled. And Charity? Ah, comes a voice as haunting as sweet music, Father Judge would tell you, "There is no lovelier word in literature, sacred or profane, than Charity."

With my whole heart I have sought after thee
(Ps. 118, 10)

CHAPTER FIVE

It is harder than ever now to follow him. There can be no sequence of time or place. For him time was truly a myth. "The Church moves slowly. We are in no hurry," he would tell you. A month—two months was for him possibly a day—maybe two days. A wait of a minute might lengthen into hours. It made no difference to Father Judge. His patience was inexhaustible. He could become indignant with the indignation flashing from his eyes, but he would never lose his head. Never did he get discouraged. He waited for God's assistance in all things.

"Father," he was asked one day, "don't you ever get discouraged at the continual procession of hard luck?" He did not hesitate in his reply. It came like the shot of a gun. "Never! If I should let myself get discouraged for one single instant I would be licked. Discouragement is pride."

You could not hurry him to a decision. It was just impossible. His prudence might have been excessive, but once his mind was made up he went straight ahead. He would wait for a sign from God. What seemed impossible because of its insurmountable obstacles or gloomy outlook was for him the test of certitude. Remember he had cautioned his children that they were to seek the abandoned places and abandoned causes. He does not want them to become famous or renowned, but rather they are to glide in and out among the poor of body and soul, and when the empire of the Church has been built up in one place so that others may carry it on, they will be off to more desolate missions. His own children must be mindful of the future of the Church. And like the Church they must not live in a narrow, present world, but must think with Her, and build for the future.

With the eyes of faith, and with a heart

inflamed with the innumerable and untold mysteries of God's Love and Goodness as contained in the expression, "Divine Providence," Father Judge saw upon a distant hill the magnificent ideal of One Fold and One Shepherd. Humbly he crept toward it, leading his sons and his daughters; telling them they are never to be more rich than Jesus Christ; telling them that Christ would nourish them with celestial food; setting the pace and example—and offering proof of Divine favor by the progress of the Cenacle bark amid torrents of adversity. Never could he escape the Divine Image.

The Hound of Heaven beat against the doors of his conscience; duty, clear as crystal, immune from fear and human respect, pursued him down his nights and days, and kept him mournfully sensitive to a White Host raised, and some do not see. To the splash of Blood, and some do not hear. To the plague of sin, and some do not flee. To the pain of fire, and some do not fear.

.   .   .   .

Meantime with the passing of the years, his responsibilities and problems increased. He was asked to draw up rules for the Communities. The groups that had gathered around him lived out their rule of life long before they ever saw it in print. Long before the rule was begun he told his followers, "Your daily life, the practices you are given, the customs you are being taught, and the habits you are acquiring, your rule when it is written will not be different from these."

Religious habits had to be adopted. He referred the question of what kind, and of what fashion to the Holy Ghost, and he writes to his spiritual sons, "You will not forget to place this matter before the Immaculate Virginal Mother of Jesus, whose servant you wish to be. Rest assured that your choice will be very personal to her. It is she who gave Our Blessed Lord the garment of humanity and who later clothed Him in the first religious garb. 'Now the coat was without seam, woven from top throughout.'"

Then before he could realize it, his Communities received the approval of the Holy See for their canonical erection. He found himself the Founder of two Religious Communities, while he was still a member of the Congregation of the Mission. Difficulties arose. What was he to do? Long before he had said, "I wish all the joys and blessings that go with living with my confreres, I wish at the same time to remain faithful to any particular providence that God may have over me."

But this was in the beginning; what about now? That is a story that perhaps will only be told in Heaven. It was never solved during his life. His Vincentian Superiors had given him fullest sympathy and coöperation. He was an obedient son. He was bound to them with ties that are sacred and deep. He had been trained by saintly Vincentians and he loved his confreres. He had started out as a young priest to follow in the footsteps of Saint Vincent. Like Saint Vincent he wanted to empty himself and be clothed in Jesus Christ. In the livery of his King he sought to lead the lost sheep from fields of misunderstanding and ignorance into the meadow of Faith.

Just when he might have enjoyed the filial assistance of his very own priests whom he had trained and brought to the altar with his fatherly zeal and love; just a few months previous to the ordination of two more of his own sons, he heard a summons from his God Who had made the beautiful sunsets in the Berkshire hills. He thought that there was much to do. He yearned for greater and more good. But he placed his hand in the Hand of God—and went, and understood.

The zeal of thy house hath eaten me up
(*St. John 2, 17*)

CHAPTER SIX

The last two years of his life were endless days and nights of mental and physical suffering. It was the final spiritualization of a saintly soul. Even before this he had been subjected to severe trials and physical infirmities. His poor tired lungs that held out so long, with such pain and discomfort that only God knew, began to give more serious trouble. But he would not rest. He could not rest. There were vital problems to solve. The burdens were his to carry, and all who helped were only as Simon, the Cyrenian, with the lighter end of the Cross.

He returned to Holy Trinity, Alabama, for Christmas, 1931, but left for the North right after the New Year to direct and to counsel a financial campaign for funds to carry on his missions. In February of that year he was present at the ordination of another of his young men. Immediately afterward he left for Puerto Rico. He stayed on the Island until his health would permit it no longer, returning to the States during the summer.

With the autumn of 1932 the members of his spiritual families had increased to such numbers that he felt it was a personal duty to conduct intensive retreats among all the Missionary Cenacles. He gave conference after conference and insisted that all be present. He recounted the early days, and recalled the beginnings of the Institute. He cautioned his children to trust and hope and confide in the good God. The world-wide misery and poverty weighed upon him. He saw it everywhere he went. He heard the distressful cries of those who were sick in body and soul. His heart was torn for the destitute poor.

"My dear Brothers," he writes, "we cannot be insensible to the terrible sorrow that is falling upon so many. Remember this awful picture of human afflictions is neither imaginary nor overdrawn; unfortunately daily experience attest only too sadly to its dreadful reality. Not one of us can be indifferent, not even heedless to this gripping picture of human destitution, and something is demanded of us even more than the sigh of compassion or the tear of sympathy. We must make self-sacrifice until it hurts. We must cherish the thought that thousands and thousands have a claim on the crust we are eating and the piece of cloth we are wearing."

Again he returned to Holy Trinity, Alabama for Christmas, 1932. Problems awaited him there and he met and settled them. His children saw his fading skin, the tired eyes. They noticed the slowness of his step, and in the hearts of all at that time a fear arose. "Father, he is worn out, and sick." He left Holy Trinity, January 12, 1933 to return North again. In many minds the thought was present, would he ever return to Holy Trinity? He was destined to do so on one brief, hurried visit, a month later, but the scene at his departure this January 12 will never be forgotten. He made his visit to chapel.

When he came out all his children were there, kneeling, some on the stone, some on the road waiting to receive his fatherly blessing. He blessed them, and was gone, and all knew that he did not want to leave Holy Trinity that afternoon. He had postponed his departure from day to day, until at last he had to leave in the performance of duty.

In the North he went from Missionary Cenacle to Missionary Cenacle, guiding, observing, and asking questions, giving conferences and insisting on prayer and still more prayer. Puerto Rico called to him from across the sea, and on March 28, 1933, he left once more for the Island and the children there whom he loved with sincere compassion. This was to be his last visit. He remained in Puerto Rico from March until August, arriving back

in the States on August 14, the Vigil of the
Assumption.

Many of his sons and daughters met him at
the boat and were shocked by his appearance.
He was but a shadow of himself. His flashing
eyes were dimmed by the sorrow he had witnessed in Puerto Rico, but his voice was still
vibrant and full of Faith and Hope, Charity
and Peace. He gathered his children around
him in the Brooklyn Missionary Cenacle and
for an hour and a half gave what proved to be
his last conference. He admitted for the first
time since his ordination that he must take a
rest, but was optimistic about his health.

He appointed one of his own as his vicar,
with authority to speak in his name while he
went away to regain his strength. He told
them of the work that had been done and vast
things were still to be accomplished. He
pointed out how God had sustained the work,
else how could it have possibly continued? He
recounted the Cenacle principles and virtues.
"Be peaceful," he said again. "Peace is

[111]

essential for our work. Every sacrifice must be made to establish peace, save the sacrificing of principles!"

Then he told them once again the story of youth: "I have great compassion for the young," he said. "They do not know what mistakes they are making." For a time he remained at Holy Trinity Heights, Silver Spring, Maryland, and then upon the advice of his doctor entered Providence Hospital in Washington, D. C., which is under the direction of the Sisters of Charity.

Long ago he had said that it was a privilege to bear a cross and that he prayed to God to send him suffering. The three months from August 27 until November 23 were the answer to his prayers. He suffered silently and in patience. He apologized for the burden he had become, and said, "When I am well, I am going to be more considerate of the sick. The poor sick—God help them!" More considerate? He who had taught that all sick are to be given first attention!

If he were allowed to walk a little in his room it would be three times in honor of the Holy Trinity, or seven times in honor of the Seven Gifts. If you asked him how he was feeling he would say, "Now you must tell me." When told he could not go up on the roof because it was snowing, he said, "Ah, but the children love it." Another time he said, "And I am going to spend more time with my confreres when I am well." In this remark we see a heart torn between two loves: his confreres of the Congregation of the Mission and his confreres of the Most Holy Trinity.

His superiors state that he must have known that his peculiar position could not go on indefinitely. What would he have done if he were forced to make a decision between his mother Community, the Vincentians, and his spiritual children of both Communities who had grouped themselves around him and were proud to call him Father? No one can answer this question definitely. We feel that he would never renounce his allegiance to the successors of Saint Vincent, and yet we wonder how could he possibly give up the charge which seemed to be so much of God.

As his illness lengthened he drew closer to Jesus. It was hard for him to remain in bed. He would tell those who cared for him that he thought he should keep going; there was so much to be done for God and souls. He admitted that he was too sick to pray, but said, "I've made a contract with God. All I have to do is say Jesus. I cannot pray, for I'm sick; in fact I suffer more than you think I do. But Jesus understands."

A Carmelite nun sent a chaplet of the Child Jesus to the hospital. He loved it, touched it to all his medicines and sent word to all the Missionary Cenacles that they should say it daily. Often through the night he would enquire the time and then speak as if an audience were before him, "The Chalices are flashing in Rome; they are uplifted, put your intentions in."

The Baby Jesus came closer to him as he

[114]

drew closer to the Baby Jesus. Lying there without strength of body, but with his mind as ever alert to the problems of the Church and the multitudes of children, he thought only of what he could do further with his poor emaciated body to help the cause. He himself was physically spent. He knew he could do nothing. He says, "I cannot pray," and so he dictated a letter with orders that it should be given to each of his spiritual sons and daughters, that they may know that their Father is with them in spirit.

He does not enquire the feast. He knows that it is the day on which the Church chants the praises of Blessed John Gabriel Perboyre, a Vincentian martyr to China. Blessed Perboyre had often been the subject of his meditation—and back in the shadows where destiny hides, waiting for the light of Divine Providence to bring it forth, we wonder if there is not some unforged link that will connect these two Vincentians that each may show forth the glory of the other. It is our prayer that

Blessed Perboyre soon will be raised to the altar. Father Judge loved his crucified confrere, and many important events in his life and the life of his two Communities are dated on the feast of this illustrious son of Saint Vincent, who long ago was strapped to a tree of martyrdom. He had spoken of him often—and now:

Feast of Blessed John Gabriel Perboyre
1933

My dear Children:

> May the grace and peace of the
> Holy Ghost be with us forever!

I take this opportunity, on the feast of Blessed John Gabriel Perboyre, a Vincentian Martyr to China, to send my blessing and most affectionate greetings to my beloved children, recommending the zeal and great charity of this missionary, who so illuminated the Church in China. Remember, you are missionaries related to Blessed John spiritually.

I urge you strongly that all of you cherish a particular devotion to the Little

Jesus, the "Word Made Flesh." We wish the world to follow Him. Remember what you have been taught, that as far as you can you must see and realize that the child belongs to Jesus. Tell Him you wish to do much for Him and commit all things to the Holy Ghost and Most Adorable Trinity and the Holy Family, including myself. God bless you all.

If it pleases our Little Jesus to hear our prayers to give us health and strength we would be particularly zealous to do all in our power to see to it that the children of the world follow Him. Remember, we must get the child for Jesus.

Again, God bless you and love you all. May the Triune God bless and love you and may the Holy Family shelter you. You were very close to me in my prayers and thoughts on the Feast of Christ the King. I need say no more. We must ever be as close.

When it pleases Christ the King to let me come back to you all again I shall tell you the story divine and miraculous of the uplifted cup filled with the Precious

[117]

Blood. I have placed all of you in this chalice close to Jesus.

God love and bless my children. Pray for

Father

It was his last message. There was no warning then that death was so near. Apparently he was improving. Once during the night before he died he said, "Did the Baby Jesus say we could go up on the roof?" Then realizing it was night he said, "I must have been dreaming." On the morning of November 23, 1933, he awoke and said, "Oh, I was arranging for all the Masses." When he realized he had spoken, he smiled, and then as usual blessed the day. He suffered intensely that morning.

About twenty minutes after two in the afternoon he finished a light lunch and having blessed and taken his medicine, asked to be allowed to rest. Quiet reigned. A few minutes before three o'clock he whispered again, "Please let me rest!" Then immediately

the Call came, sharp and clear, like the sound
of a trumpet. There was no pain or struggle.
A quick, hushed breath, the fleetest dawning
of a smile, the hand of a priest raised in final
absolution. Resting as he had asked, Father
Judge gave up his noble soul to the Triune
God and the Immaculate Lily of the Most
Holy Trinity.

The clock struck three as the Silence settled
on his tired eyes. And before the final echo
had faded into the afternoon his guardian
angel had come quietly, like the fall of silver
snow, and had whispered that the Baby Jesus
wanted him then. The spark that had kept
him body and soul was stilled, and the spirit,
released from its bodily prison, flew like a
brilliant bird to the nest of his Maker's arms.
All the little streams of his hopes, and his
yearnings, and his meditations had finally
found their outlet in the Unknown Ocean of
Desire where all floods flow.

The creature had found His Creator. The

servant, the Master. The pupil, the Supreme Teacher. The lover, the Great Beloved. The Priest, the High Priest. A man of God had found the Divinity.

Precious in the sight of the Lord
is the death of His saints
(*Ps. 115, 15*)

CHAPTER SEVEN

News of his death spread rapidly from Missionary Cenacle to Missionary Cenacle. A cable flashed the word to Puerto Rico. His sons and daughters traveling on the missions heard it as soon as modern science could get the message to them: "Father is dead." Almost immediately, like a gust of wind that shakes the fruit from the tree, the wires and mails brought testimonials of his sanctity. "By their fruits you shall know them."

The first night in death he spent with the Daughters of Saint Vincent de Paul at Providence Hospital, Washington. And he would have wished it so. Many of them remembered retreats that he had given. They recalled his early zeal and counsels. These Sisters had been a comfort to him in his last illness, and a kind Providence ordained that they should be there when this humble son of Saint Vincent left to join their spiritual Father, whom he so bravely followed.

His own children of the Missionary Cenacle watched through the night and until Friday afternoon when his body was removed to the Mother Missionary Cenacle in Philadelphia. From Friday afternoon until the hour of his funeral a continual rosary was recited. Had he not said, "Be sure to hold on to your rosary. We have to keep that moving because we need all kinds of things?"

His body lay for six days in the Mother-house of his spiritual daughters. A constant procession filed past his coffin during that time. All sorts of religious articles were pressed to his lifeless hands, and when too great a crowd would gather, those who did not have an opportunity to obtain these relics would wait patiently and ask one of the Brothers or Sisters to make sure that they touched the hands that had been so often raised in blessing. They brought flowers, too, pressed them to his body, and took them away.

A strange silence filled the chapel. Grief would sometimes give way to an audible sob. There was the never-ending procession past the bier, always you could hear, "Hail Mary— now and at the hour of our death," but for it all, the Silence pressed against you, for actually to see him in chapel with such a multitude, and not to hear again the story of the Word Made Flesh, or the Immensity of the constant drip of Precious Blood upon the world, was something that had never happened before. It was proof to his children that he was really dead!

So long as a last flickering spark of life had flamed in his soul, his mind sent messages to his heart and his heart beat furiously with love— and his love poured forth through his words —he said, "I behold you in God—Remember the child."

Tuesday night each one kept a private vigil with his Father. The melody of hope con-

tinued, "Blessed art thou among women and
blessed is the Fruit of thy womb Jesus."
Early Wednesday morning his own priests
celebrated the Divine Sacrifice, and blessed the
remains of their Founder. Time became
doubly precious. His children knew that soon
he would leave.

Memories crowded upon memories. As they
kissed his hands in farewell, they knew that
from above he would be forever blessing
them. The long sorrowful procession traveled
through the streets of Philadelphia and over
into Germantown to Saint Vincent's Seminary
where his body was met by the Fathers of the
Congregation of the Mission, and escorted
into the chapel. The casket was opened before the main altar, the Office of the Dead
recited, and then a solemn Mass of requiem
was sung.

After the Mass the scenes that had been so
touching in the Sisters' Motherhouse again
took place. The hands were kissed, rosaries
were pressed to them, and finally the chalice

which he had held aloft in life and in death, was removed from his anointed fingers and the casket closed for the last time.

The final procession started from the seminary and wound its way out to Holy Sepulchre cemetery where a place had been made for him next to the grave of Mother Boniface. Priests and Sisters and Brothers and friends closed in about the grave, a last absolution was given, the *De Profundis* was said, the *Benedictus* sung, and his body was lowered tenderly into the earth. It was the end. And yet, no, someone started the rosary. He himself would have done it had it been another whose body went down—and so all his children once more called upon the Queen of Heaven—"now and at the hour of our death."

* * *

And so the story begins. What has been set down here is only the preface. In his last will and testament he left to the world, his children; to his children, the child. And to the child who will grow as life flows on, he left a heritage of Compassionate Love that is found in the uplifted chalice filled with the Precious Blood of the Little Lord Jesus.